First published in Great Britain in 1991
by Simon & Schuster Young Books

Photoset by Goodfellow & Egan Ltd, Cambridge
Colour origination by Scantrans Pte Ltd, Singapore

Printed and bound in Belgium by Proost International Book Productions

Simon & Schuster Young Books
Simon & Schuster Ltd
Wolsey House
Wolsey Road
Hemel Hempstead HP2 4SS

BRITISH LIBRARY CATALOGUING IN PUBLICATION DATA
Ryan, Margaret
Sir Chancelot and the horrible howling monster
I. Title II. Petrone, Valeria III. Series
823'.914 [J]

ISBN 0 7500 0799 0
ISBN 0 7500 0800 8 Pbk

Margaret Ryan

Sir Chancelot and the horrible howling monster

Illustrated by Valeria Petrone

SIMON & SCHUSTER

LONDON • SYDNEY • NEW YORK • TOKYO • SINGAPORE • TORONTO

One

Sir Chancelot sat alone in the great hall of Chancet castle and sighed. He was really fed up. It was at least three days since he'd rescued anyone from drowning in a murky pool, or falling from a tall building, or slipping on a banana skin in front of a high speed train. *Ouch*! Messy one that.

"I hope someone needs my help soon," he said. "I'm getting really fed up. What's the point of being a knight in shining armour if no one needs my help?"

He was just thinking about beginning a tiddly wink tournament when there was a small tap on the great hall door.

"That's funny," he said. "I don't remember that tap being there before . . ."

McPeevish, his butler, entered.

“Ah, McPeevish,” said Sir Chancelot. “Have you brought me any news? Is there a daring deed that I can do? Is there a mighty task for me to perform? Is there —”

“There is a letter, sire,” said McPeevish. “Shall I read it out?”

Sir Chancelot nodded.

“It's from some villagers in distress.”

“Distress?” said Sir Chancelot. “I don't think I know that place. Is it near here?”

McPeevish sighed. Sometimes being Sir Chancelot's butler was not an easy job.

"It seems," McPeevish continued, "that a horrible howling monster is roaming through the woods beside the village of Little Pimple-on-the-Nose. The villagers are afraid to go out at night, their hens are too scared to lay eggs, and their cows have stopped giving milk. No one has actually caught sight of the monster because it only starts its horrible howling when it's dark, but the villagers have seen prints of its huge clawed feet."

"The monster gives a horrible howl, you say?" said Sir Chancelot. "I wonder what that sounds like. Would it be an *OOOH-EEEH-OUCH* kind of howl?"

"More horrible than that, sire," said McPeevish.

Sir Chancelot paced up and down, deep in thought. "How about an *AHL-WAHL-YAHL?*"

"Even more horrible than that, sire," said McPeevish.

Sir Chancelot paced up and down even deeper in thought. Then he accidentally tripped over the tiddly wink board, fell flat, and banged his nose on the tiled floor.

"*OWL-YOWL-WOWL!*" he howled.

"You've got it now, sire," beamed McPeevish, checking with the letter. "That's the horrible howl exactly. Now, can you help the villagers get rid of the monster?"

Sir Chancelot got up from the floor, holding his nose. "Held? Ob course, I ban held. Seb for the yebbow ages."

"Pardon?" said McPeevish.

Sir Chancelot took his hand away from his nose.

"Of course I can help. Send for the Yellow Pages. Right away."

Two

McPeevish put his fingers to his lips and gave a loud whistle: *WHEEEEE EEEEEEE WEEEEEEP*.

The Yellow Pages appeared. There were three of them: Page One, Page Two and Page Three. They wore yellow tunics, yellow tights, yellow boots and yellow hats, and they looked . . . yellow.

They swept Sir Chancelot a low bow (they also swept the castle stairs, but only on Fridays).

"You sent for us, sire," they said. All at once. At the same time. Together.

"Yes," said Sir Chancelot. "We're off to help some villagers in distress." And he told them about the letter.

McPeevish brought Sir Chancelot and the Yellow Pages a map. "I've marked the spot where Little Pimple-on-the-Nose is with a cross," he said. "Just follow the motorway till you see a big sign saying *Little Pimple-on-the-Nose*, and turn left."

"Right," said Page One.

"Right right," said Page Two.

"OK," said Page Three.

"But how do we get to the motorway?" asked Sir Chancelot, who wasn't very good with maps.

"Bottom of the garden, turn left," said McPeevish, who then went off to his pantry to polish his silver and iron his ten pound notes.

Meanwhile Sir Chancelot was considering the question of transport.

"Now, Yellow Pages," he said. "We must consider the question of transport."

"Let's take our jet-propelled skateboards," said Page One.

"I think our skateboards would be best," said Page Two.

"Our skateboards are the answer," said Page Three.

"I know what we'll do about transport," said Sir Chancelot. "We'll take our jet-propelled skateboards. Follow me, Yellow Pages . . . TO THE RESCUE!"

They found the motorway quite easily by sneaking round the back of the pansy patch, creeping past the lupins, and tip-toeing down the long front drive to the garden gate.

The motorway was busy with cars, buses and lorries all jammed up going nowhere.

"This is no use," said Sir Chancelot. "We'll never get to the villagers in Little Pimple-on-the-Nose at this rate. Switch on jet engines to full power, Yellow Pages. This is an emergency."

"Skateboard One switched on, and taking off now, sire," said Page One.

WHOOOOOOOOSH!

And it rose into the air.

"Skateboard Two switched on, and taking off now, sire," said Page Two.
WHOOOOOSH . . .
WHOOOOOOSH!

"Skateboard Three switched on, and taking off now, sire," said Page Three.
WHOOOOO
WHOOOOO
WHOOOOO . . . SH!

And all three Yellow Pages were in the air.

"Chancelot Airways boarding now," said Sir Chancelot. "Please have your boarding cards ready."

Then he missed the switch, slipped, and fell off his skateboard on to the grass verge.

Sir Chancelot's face was purple pink as he stepped back on to his skateboard, but this time he found the switch, and he too roared *WHOOOOOOOOOOSH* into the air. The Yellow Pages had throttled back to hover speed to wait for him, and they all finally zoomed off. *To the rescue*!

Three

After a while, the rescuers saw a big road sign that said:

then another sign appeared that said:

then a third sign appeared that said:

Eventually Sir Chancelot and the Yellow Pages found the village. Unfortunately Sir Chancelot overshot the village green and ended up in the village pond in among the ducks.

"Don't be frightened, little ducks," he told them. "It's just old Uncle Chancelot come to visit. I won't harm you."

"Who is this guy?" asked a duck with a green head.

"Don't know," said another. "Probably a quackpot."

Sir Chancelot rescued his skateboard and waded out of the pond. Emptying his waterlogged boots, he looked about. There wasn't a soul to be seen. The village was empty and silent. No faces appeared at the windows; no heads looked out of the doors.

"Poor villagers," said Sir Chancelot. "They must be too afraid of the horrible howling monster to come out. Look, even the ducks have gone off indoors now. This cannot go on. I shall inform them that now I am here, they have nothing to fear."

Sir Chancelot stood in the middle of the empty village square and shouted, "Good villagers, don't be afraid! I, the great Sir Chancelot, have come to help you, and rid you of this horrible howling monster. With the aid of my rusty Yellow Pages . . ."

"*Trusty* Yellow Pages," muttered Page One.

" . . . Sorry, *trusty* Yellow Pages, I shall track the monster down, tie him up and carry him off. Do not be afraid. Come on out!"

Not one villager came out, but instead old boots and shoes and kettles came flying from windows and doorways, and Sir Chancelot had to duck to avoid them. Then a voice called out, "Will you quit yelling out there! Don't you know our favourite programme is on the telly?"

Once the programme had finished, the villagers came out and told Sir Chancelot and the Yellow Pages all about the horrible howling monster.

"He howls something horrible," they said. "We're too scared to go out at night, and the cows are too scared to give milk, and the hens are too scared to lay eggs. The monster starts off howling with a bit of yowling, then moaning with a bit of groaning, followed by crying with a bit of sighing, and finally a double helping of yelping."

Sir Chancelot looked thoughtful. "Tell you what we'll do. Tonight, when the moon is full, the Yellow Pages and I will lie in wait in that wood on the edge of the village, and when the horrible howling monster appears we'll catch him."

"And snatch him," said Page One.

"And dispatch him," said Page Two.

"Pity about those hens," said Page Three. "I love toast soldiers with my boiled egg."

Four

That night, when they were all full of toast soldiers with no eggs and tea with no milk, Sir Chancelot and the Yellow Pages lay in wait in the dark and rustling wood. Sir Chancelot had wrapped himself in a big tartan rug – he did not like to be a cold knight.

"I hope this lying in wait doesn't take too long," said Page One. "I've got a crick in my neck."

"I've got a rick in my back," said Page Two.

"I've got a tick in my watch," said Page Three.

"Don't talk so much," said Sir Chancelot. "Listen! Did you hear something?"

"No," said Page One.

"No," said Page Two.

"No," said Page Three.

"Neither did I," said Sir Chancelot.

Suddenly they heard a very strange noise. There was a howling with a bit of yowling, a moaning with a bit of groaning, a crying with a bit of sighing, and a double helping of yelping.

"Come on, Yellow Pages," said Sir Chancelot. "Follow me!"

He stood up and tripped over the rug.
"No way," muttered the Yellow Pages.

Sir Chancelot stood up again. "Bring the rug," he said. "We'll use it to throw over the monster."

Silently . . . well, nearly silently . . . well, not very silently . . . well, quite noisily really, they followed the sound of the horrible howling monster who was howling with a bit of – oh you know the rest – till they came to a little clearing in the woods.

And there they saw the shadowy figure of a horrible howling monster. He was sitting on a tree stump, howling horribly.

"Quick! Throw the rug over it," said Sir Chancelot, and as a large cloud slid over the moon, he threw himself on the monster and wrestled him to the ground.

"Got you, you horrible howling monster you," he panted. "No more will the villagers be afraid to lay eggs. No more will the cows be afraid to go out at night. No more will the hens stop giving milk —"

"But, Sir Chancelot . . ." said Page One.

"But wait, Sir Chancelot . . ." said Page Two.

"Hang on a minute, Sir Chancelot," said Page Three.

"What do you think I'm doing?" puffed Sir Chancelot. "This monster's so heavy I can't move him."

"That's not the monster you've got," said Page One.

"That's the tree stump you've got. The monster jumped out of the way," said Page Two.

"We've got the monster," said Page Three. "And he's not horrible . . . he's cuddly."

"Good gracious," said Sir Chancelot. "He's a horrible howling *baby* monster."

"Who's an ickle lickle diddums, then?" Page One asked the baby monster.

"Who's a tootsie wootsie cutsie, then?" Page Two asked the baby monster.

"Who's gone and lost his mumsie-wumsie and dadsie-wadsie, then," Page Three asked the baby monster.

"I have," said the baby monster. "And it's really most upsetting."

Five

The baby monster explained that several nights ago all the monsters had gathered in the woods for a party. They'd gobbled up all the wobbly jelly and the ice-cream, then played hide-and-seek among the trees. The baby monster had crawled into a hollow log to hide, and had fallen asleep. When he woke up it was daylight and all the monsters had gone home.

"Monsters are afraid of the light," he said. "That's when the scary humans come out."

"Gosh," said Page One.

"Golly," said Page Two.

"I hadn't thought of that," said Page Three. "But weren't you cold and hungry?"

"Monsters don't feel the cold," said the baby monster. "And the cows and hens gave me all their milk and eggs. They know how hungry and thirsty monsters get."

"Well, we must get you back to your parents as soon as possible," said Sir Chancelot.

"They're in the woods somewhere," said the baby monster. "I can hear them howling in the distance. I howl back, but they can't hear me." And he began to cry. A horrible howling cry. "*OWL WOWL YOWL . . .*"

"Oh, don't do that," said Page One, giving him her hanky.

"We'll find your mum and dad," said Page Two.

"But how?" said Page Three.

"Ahem ahem," said Sir Chancelot. "Just leave this to me." He sat the baby monster back up on the tree stump then put his fingers to his lips and gave a loud whistle. *WHEEEEE EEEEE WEEEEEP*.

"McPeevish taught me to do that," he said. "It's bound to bring the monsters here. Now let's hide behind those bushes and watch. We don't want to scare the monsters away."

A few moments later there was a hashing and a bashing and a crashing through the woods, and two enormous monsters appeared in the clearing.

"Baby monster!" they cried and ran to their long-lost son. They gave him two monster hugs each. *CRUNCH CRUNCH. CRUNCH CRUNCH.*

"Mummy monster. Daddy monster," the baby cried, and gave them two monster kisses back. *SLURP. SLURP.*

Behind the bushes Sir Chancelot beamed. "Another successful mission, Yellow Pages," he said. "Now we can return to Chancet castle."

"Right," said Page One, and zoomed off on her skateboard.

"Right right," said Page Two, and zoomed off on her skateboard.

"Right right right," said Page Three and zoomed off on his skateboard.

"Now where did I leave my skateboard?" said Sir Chancelot. "It must be around here somewhere . . . Don't go without me, Yellow Pages. There are horrible howling monsters in this wood . . ."

"*OWWWWWWWWWL WOWWWWWWWWL YOWWWWWWWL . . .*"